SEQUOIA
KINGS CANYON
national parks

SEQUOIA
KINGS CANYON
national parks

Designed, Written, and Edited by
Randy Collings

Published for and in behalf of Guest Services, Inc.
by

ADAM RANDOLPH COLLINGS
incorporated

Box 8658 Holiday Station, Anaheim, California 92802

Cover: Sequoiandendron Giganteum by Mark Miller
— Mount Whitney by Pat O'Hara.
Opening spreads in order: Kings Canyon High
Country by William Tweed — Sequoias in un-
named grove by David Muench — spring in
Sierra foothills by William Tweed — American
black bear by Dave Garber — sunset from
Sequoia National Park by Lyn Radeka.

Middle
Fork

Kings Canyon

Kings
River

Volcanic
Lakes

National Park

Mist
Falls

Kings River
Canyon

Cedar
Grove

Grant Grove Village

Muir
Grove

Giant
Forest

Mount
Whitney •
14,495 ft.

Sequoia National Park

Kern
River

Mineral
King •

North

0 1 2 3 4 5
Miles

Giant Sequoias

SEQUOIA
KINGS CANYON
national parks

DISCOVERY: 1858

SET APART: Sequoia—by an act of Congress on September
                  25, 1890
                  Kings Canyon—by an act of Congress on
                  March 4, 1940

LOCATION: From an elevation of 1,700 on the western face
                  of the Sierra Nevada Mountains in central Cali-
                  fornia to the crest of that range at 14,495 feet.

SIZE: approximately 900 square miles.

One hundred million years ago things were far different from the world in which we live today. The Age of Reptiles was at its height. Huge dinosaurs lumbered over the land. Strange sea monsters swarmed in the seas. Bizarre lizard-like birds filled the skies. Were you or I able to witness such a scene first hand we would fail to recognize much of anything. Yet gazing out across this primeval landscape of volcanic activity and primitive vegetation we would find, towering above the head of the Tyrannosaurus Rex, a sight familiar to those who have traveled in modern day California. There on the horizon, a noble form would greet the eye: Massive wall of timber covered in that unmistakable cloak of soft cinnamon colored bark — juniper-like limbs forming a crown to grace its upper reaches; the Sequoiandendron giganteum, California's giant redwood, flourishing in ancient forests across the globe.

Scientists reason that it was the great Ice Age that brought about the almost complete demise of a tree God had designed to live forever.

Along the western coast of North America shifting continental plates had caused a great uplift to occur. Rising gently on the West then dropping off suddenly like a wall on the East the mighty Sierra Nevada mountain range came into being. This same buckling action caused the creation of the Sierra's Latin sister, the Andes. As the land rose it carried with it vegetation and wildlife. It was a slow transition. Many years have transpired as the mountain building process continues even today.

By the time these mighty mountains had shuffled into position the earth itself had begun to shift on its axis. Great sheets of ice, glaciers, blanketed much of the planet. Polar ice caps extended southward and northward to encompass vast regions of once temperate life zones. Rivers of ice flowed down from the crest of the new mountains, scouring out valleys, gouging canyon walls, transforming jagged peaks into domes and arches.

Through it all there remained, in isolated recesses of the Sierra Range, small groves of sequoias, where the icy fingers of death did not reach. Warm currents of air rushed up from regions now familiar to us as Southern California, abating the ferocity of the arctic onslaught.

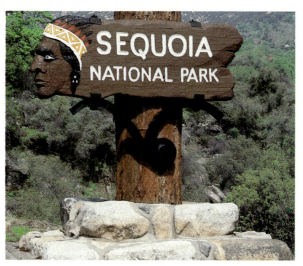

A *living relic* from the Dinosaur Age (previous page), Sequoias, such as the General Grant Tree (left), remain today only in isolated recesses of California's Sierra Nevada Mountains.

As the glaciers themselves finally gave way and began to melt they left behind the incomparable landscapes of Yosemite and Kings Canyon. The rivers of ice also took with them countless species of animal and plant life, vanished forever from off the face of the earth. Gone were the giant mammoths and cave bear. Gone were the warm inland seas and tropical vegetation that at one time covered much of North America.

As the frosts and fogs cleared from the face of the land, one lone survivor remained. Reduced to a mere handful in number, the tenacious sequoia still clung to life, eradicated from the face of the earth, save it were a few fragile groves on the gentle Western slope of the Sierra escarpment.

It is not known for certain when man first came upon the scene. Archaeologists speculate that his arrival in the Sierra Country predate the birth of Christ by about 2,000 years. Local Potwisha Indians were familiar with the giant forests hidden away in the mountains above their villages. During warm summer months they migrated to the ancient groves to escape the heat and drought-like summer conditions still prevalent today in the San Joaquin Valley.

Years of Spanish occupation in California had done little to disrupt life amongst the In-

dians of the area's interior. Few explorations were conducted. Those that were seemed confined to coastal areas and directed at purposes of colonization rather than scientific study. The Americanization of the West Coast El Dorado, however, brought total disruption to the idyllic pastoral life-style of the native population.

As in the Andes, the Sierra's proved to be a virtual treasure chest of gold. Unlike the people of ancient South America, native Californians had either not discovered the precious metal or more probably found little use for it. Hence the treasure lay buried in silt, where glacial runoff had deposited it many thousands of years earlier. Its discovery instigated one of the greatest mass migrations of people and cultures that the world had ever experienced. For the first time in recorded history attention was focused on the vast unexplored territory of California's mighty Sierra Nevadas. Forty-niner's struck with gold fever, poured over the mountain passes and out of countless ships, by the thousands.

Initial discoveries had been made in the Sierra foothills near Sacramento. As competition and claim-jumping increased, fortune seekers began pushing further and further back into the mountains. During the decade that fol-

lowed one startled miner after another stumbled upon grove after grove of the magnificient prehistoric trees. In 1852 A.T. Dowd, a hungry miner chasing after a wounded bear stumbled into the realm of the giants at Calaveras grove. Subsequent discoveries were frequent although most fell upon disbelieving ears.

To the South near the present day city of Visalia came a one time Forty-niner turned rancher by the name of Hale Tharp. Tharp was an amicable sort of fellow. The local Indians accepted him as one of their own. Tharp became especially endeared to the Potwisha Chief Chappo himself.

One summer's morning while running his cattle near Three Rivers, the Yankee settler was invited by Chief Chappo and his braves to view something that the Indians most certainly considered sacred.

Escorting the white brother they began to climb from the wooded hillsides of oak and sycamore to the shadowy forests of ponderosa and incense cedar. They climbed the steep trail past gigantic Moro Rock and then to the amazement of the startled Tharp gazed upon what is today known as Giant Forest, our portal to the most extensive expanse of Sequoiandendron gigan-

The Loghouse of Hale Thorp (below) still stands near Crescent Meadow in Sequoia National Park. John Muir (left), one of America's most beloved naturalists.

19

teum on the face of the earth. Tharp most assuredly had heard tales of the awesome trees further north from many a miner. But here stretched one grove after another, indeed an entire forest graced by these ancient towering monarchs.

From that summer till the day Tharp died he spent his life amongst the noble giants, fashioning a home out of the hollow of a fallen Sequoia near Crescent Meadow (Tharp's redwood home is still on exhibit there today). Some years later John Muir, father of the Yosemite and one of America's greatest advocates for conservation, visited him in what Muir called Tharp's "noble den." Muir and others did much to attract national attention towards the soon to be endangered trees.

Muir loved the high Sierra country. He called it the "Range of Light" perhaps because of the blinding glow it casts as the sun reflects off perennial snow banks and glacier-polished domes. Scottish born and largely self-educated, Muir came to a crossroads in his life after a bout with blindness. He forsook the opportunity of becoming a multi-millionaire as an inventor and entrepreneur and chose instead the life of a mountain-man. "One day I set off to take a walk in the woods," as he tells it, "and I never came back."

Upon his arrival in San Francisco in 1868, he questioned a local as to where the wild country was. His informer obliged by pointing to the East. Muir hiked from the floor of California's Central Valley up into the High Sierra for the first time. He became ecstatic when he beheld the incredulous beauty of Yosemite Valley. His further experience among the Sierra's mighty redwoods caused him to define his "giants grouped in temple groves" as "Kings of the Conifers of the world — the noblest of a noble race."

When a sawmill was located nine miles from Tharp's Giant Forest, public-spirited citizens, encouraged by the writings of John Muir, pushed for the establishment of a federal reserve to protect the area from exploitation.

The result of their efforts came on September 25, 1890 in the form of a bill signed into action by President Benjamin Harrison creating Sequoia National Park as the nation's second such reserve. Yellowstone had been formed just eight years before while Yosemite at the time was under the protection of a California initiated ordinance.

Felling a giant (below). Early illustration of the Sequoia (right).

VIEW IN THE SIERRA FOREST.

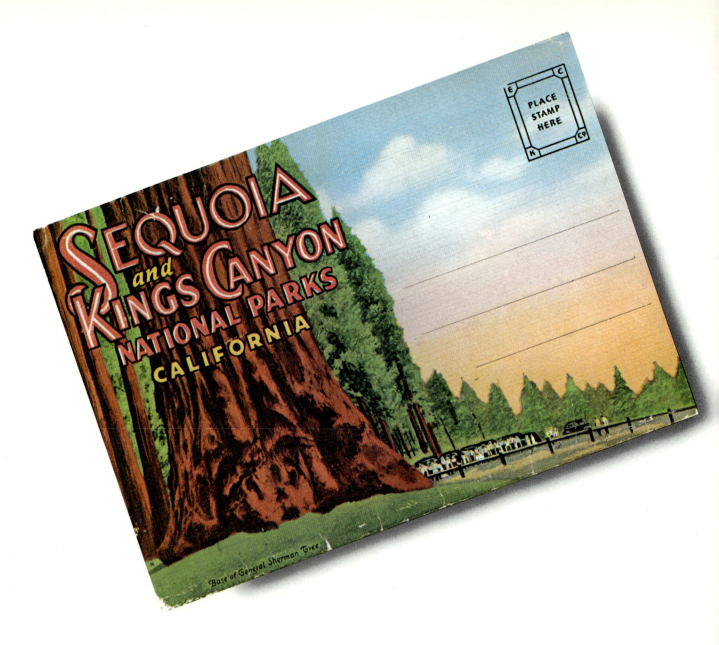

PLACE STAMP HERE

SEQUOIA and KINGS CANYON NATIONAL PARKS CALIFORNIA

Base of General Sherman Tree

PHOTO BY LINDLEY EDDY STUDIOS   SEQUOIA NATIONAL PARK, CALIFORNIA

"OLD SCARFACE"

119535

Fascinated by tales of Hale Tharp's Giant Forest, visitors from then until now have flocked to these groves of ancient Sequoias. Some come to satisfy curiosity; others to worship and reflect.

Today Sequoia and King's Canyon plays host to more than 2.5 million guests annually. All are served by the attentive National Park Service employees and gracious hospitality of GSI (Guest Services, Incorporated) the twin park's concessionaire.

403   THE AUTO LOG, SEQUOIA NATIONAL PARK, CALIFORNIA

120186

President Harrison, whose private ambition had been to set aside Arizona's Grand Canyon for the enjoyment of the people, which he did soon after formulation of the Sequoia reserve, chose Secretary of the Interior William Noble's suggestion to name the park after the trees for which it had been established to protect. The giant trees themselves had been named by an Austrian botanist probably in honor of Chief Seqoyah, a giant among the Cherokee Indians who had done much to assist his people by developing for them an alphabet.

Three weeks after Sequoia National Park came into being the General Grant Grove nearby was also set aside. In 1940 a stretch of spectacular glacial-formed geography which surrounded the General Grant National Park, known as Kings Canyon, was also designated as a reserve. This region received its name from Spanish explorers who christened the river that flowed from within this mountain throne room after the Three Wise Men, Holy Kings, who came to visit the boy child Jesus in Bethlehem. Today the two stand side by side, each as hallmarks to the idealism and foresight of the American people.

The Sequoiandendron giganteum is one of three known species of redwood to have survived the march of time. Related redwoods remain along the northern coast of California. Sequoia's second cousin, the dawn redwood, is found only in an isolated region of Central China.

Within the groves of Sequoia and Kings Canyon National Parks stand several thousand giant sequoias. They are the largest of all living things and indeed among the oldest. The General Sherman tree for instance, boasts a base circumference of 102 feet. One hundred twenty feet above the ground, the trunk is still 17 feet through. Largest of all Sequoia, hence the largest living thing on earth, General Sherman towers 272 feet above the ground. As tall as this may seem it would be well to note that some

Parker Grove of giant Sequoias (right)
Dogwood (below)

Largest living thing in the world, General Sherman (left and below) dominate surrounding groves of redwoods.

It seems an impossibility, yet the mighty Sequoia begins life as a tiny cone about the size of a grain of wheat. Producing both male and female elements the giant redwood's reproductive sequence begins in mid-to-late winter when golden clouds of pollen are released from the male cones to fertilize the tiny female cones.

Mature seed-bearing cones are about 2.5 inches long. Some 400,000 seeds are released from each tree every year. Of them only a few will ever become seedlings (next page). Even fewer will survive to become monarchs of the forest.

Winter in Giant Forest (previous page and these pages). Here cross-country skiing is a favorite activity.

PHOTOGRAPHS: BILL ROSS

Sierra winters shroud the forest in a regal cloak of white. Although open year round at Giant Forest, regions beyond are often accessible only to the snowmobile or skier.

LODGEPOLE
VISITOR CENTER

INFORMATION   EXHIBITS
RANGER   STATION

Lost Grove (previous page and left). The president tree (below) towers some 200 feet above the forest.

–It is difficult for the mind to fathom the gigantic size of these noble trees. When common objects such as automobiles are combined with the primeval scene as here at this popular fallen monarch (below) near Crescent Meadow, we grasp the full magnitude of the giant's dimensions.

ED COOPER

40

species of the coast redwood have been known to attain well over 350 feet in height. Yet none have come close to the astounding girth of their Sierra brothers. The General Sherman tree was discovered by James Wolverton, a trooper since employed by Hale Tharp as a ranc hand, who named the massive living monument in honor of his civil war commander, William T. Sherman.

In Kings Canyon stands the twin park's second most famous monarch, the General Grant tree (actually six feet larger at the base yet somewhat smaller in overall volume than the General Sherman). General Sherman and General Grant come about as close to eternity as

any mortal thing can. They have each been standing for well over 2,000 years. Life for them began at the height of the Egyptian Civilization. By the time Rome was founded they had attained their youthful lanky profile. Each appeared much as they do today when Columbus discovered America. To stand at the base of either Monarch is to feel at one with eternity.

In far recesses of Sequoia National Park there are many other trees who challenge the longevity of these two giants.

There are several reasons for the long life of the Sequoia. The bark which clothes the trunk of the tree is extremely thick and almost impervious to fire. Within the bark itself much of

Spring arrives late in Crescent Meadow (left). Wildflowers such as the Tiger Lily (above), Shooting Star (middle) and Lupine (below) bloom through August.

the life functions of the tree are carried out. Tannic acid from inside protects the redwood from insect infestation. It is not uncommon to see specimens that have been completely hollowed by fire, yet they continue to thrive because of the tree's persistent bark. Indeed most every monarch is marred by fire as well one might expect, since they stand vulnerable for thousands of years to the onslaught of lightning as they tower above all else in the forest.

Nature has provided this remnant of the dinosaur age with every conceivable protection. No one has ever seen a dying redwood. Time and the elements eventually topple them. Once uprooted, and only then, they pass away, their skeleton lying intact upon the ground for another thousand years.

Except for the Ice Age, which obliterated the trees global range, man has posed to the Sequoia's their only threat. The extensive groves of Sequoia Kings Canyon National Parks don't begin to match the vast Sequoia forest that was still intact just a century ago. Prior to the formation of the twin parks, logging operations destroyed much of the finest forest of Sequoia in the world, an extensive expanse containing at least four giants that were even bigger than General Sherman.

Today under the protection of State and Federal government these magnificent groves of trees will continue to flourish thousands of years after you and I are gone.

The Sequoiandendron giganteum forest today thrive at between 5,000 to 8,000 feet. This is a region where the winters are somewhat gentle when compared with higher elevations. It is a timberzone that is bathed with perennial sunlight and an abundance of ground water — all elements essential to the perpetration of redwood.

The beauty of the Mariposa Lily (below) and the grandeur of mighty Sequoia (right).

BILL ROSS

WM. TWEED

Fog frequently enshrouds the Sequoia forest, particularly during winter months (previous page). Magnificent Moro Rock (above), Crystal Cave (left) are popular visitor attractions in the twin parks.

High above the groves rise the lofty summits of the Sierra Nevada. This mass of mountain is greater than the extensive alpine system of Europe combined and outside of Alaska contains the highest summits in North America (seven such peaks within Kings Canyon reach above 14,000 feet in height). Here in an arctic climate so very much in contrast with the temperate conditions for which the rest of California is famous, summer is but a brief visitor.

Kings River rushes forth from portals of the great Sierra Canyon that shares its name.

North Dome (next page) rises above a scene not unlike that of nearby Yosemite National Park.

ROY MURPHY

ROY MURPHY

Beautiful Grizzly Falls (left) in Kings Canyon waters a magnificent landscape of pine and fir. This is favorite terrain for Ursus Americanus — the American Black bear. Frequently tagged for scientific studies, the black bear (color varies from black to brown) resides here in the twin parks in substantial numbers. Back country ranger stations (right) are rustic structures constructed from local timbers.

WM. TWEED

DAVE GRABER

PHOTOGRAPHS: GUEST SERVICES, INC.

The General Grant Tree (these pages) second most popular tree in the twin parks, rises high above surrounding groves.

Racoons (left) are nocturnal. Hence they are rarely seen during day light hours. The mighty Sierra Crest (above) towers over Kern River Basin.

In this world up here, a territory that accounts for nearly 50% of Sequoia National Park and well over 75% of Kings Canyon, conditions most resemble regions of Northern Alaska. Sierran winters are severe, yielding anywhere from 250 to 440 inches of snow! Snowfall occurs year round and in upper reaches rarely, if ever completely melts away. The resulting landscape is stark. Twisted pine and tiny alpine wildflowers cling to life wherever possible. From here, on top of the world the vista's are breathtaking.

Crowning this arctic wilderness at the eastern edge stands 14,495 foot Mt. Whitney, the highest mountain in the continental United States. A favorite among hikers and backpack-

ers the summit can be reached by either the West or East side of the mountain. Accessibility to the foot of the mountain via paved road, however, is limited to Whitney Portal on the Eastern face. For this reason most who visit the parks never see Whitney. A hike to its summit is not as strenuous as one might suppose. Thousands make the climb annually. Pack mules are available from Whitney Portal.

Kings Canyon is the park for backpackers. Boasting an incredible valley not unlike that of the Yosemite, the remainder of this Mountain Land's wonders lie in the high country, accessible only by foot trails.

Bear are plentiful throughout both parks

Much of Sequoia and Kings Canyon National Parks is accessible only by trail. High country meadows (next page) and spectacular views of crystal clear mountain lakes (below), reward those who venture into the back country.

PHOTOGRAPHS: WM. TWEED

WM. TWEED

The golden trout (right) is native only to pure mountain lakes of California's Southern Sierra.

BILL ROSS

WM. TWEED

PHOTOGRAPHS: WM. TWEED

ED COOPER

Above the timberline lonely pines struggle to survive. Lakes and meadows provide more hospitable environs. Splendid Mt. Muir (next page). Towering over the grandest of Sierra peaks, Mt. Whitney (pages 76-77), at 14,495 feet, crowns a stark landscape not unlike that found in the Arctic. Here tiny flowers and snow plants bloom briefly between winters.

71

ED COOPER

WM. TWEED

PAT O'HARA

ED COOPER

WM. TWEED

75

ROY MURPHY

Those who venture into the back country are counseled to store food properly so as to avoid the problems of having uninvited dinner guests. Bighorn sheep are also present in the high country although seldom seen, as are mountain lion and bobcats.

Mule deer are a common sight throughout the forests and meadows of the Sierra Country. Racoons, Marmots, and even Wolverines (although extremely rare) all make this mountain paradise their home.

Wildlife is most abundant in the lower elevations of the National Park. Here early spring brings about one of the finest displays of green grass and wildflowers in the world. By the time she has reached the meadows of the high country the foothills have been burnished brown by the intense heat of the summer sun. Indeed this is a region typical of California where only two seasons predominate — one mild and wet, the other warm and very dry. It is here at Ash Mountain, elevation 1,700, that we find Park Headquarters. Outstanding lodging, restaurant and campgrounds are maintained throughout both parks by the National Park Service and Guest Services, Incorporated.

While visiting either park take a moment to pause and reflect upon the intrinsic value of wilderness, upon things greater than you or I, upon the dramatic and the sublime. Discover Sequoia and Kings Canyon and in so doing rediscover yourself. Renew your own inner source of strength and you will return from the mountain a better soul for having been there.

In sharp contrast to the forboding landscapes of the Sierra Crest, the gently sloping foothill regions of Sequoia National Park (these pages) sport greenery during a long rainey season and golden brown during summer months.

THE END

ADAM RANDOLPH COLLINGS
incorporated